★ UNITED STATES PRESIDENTS ★

George W. BUSH

BreAnn Rumsch

Big Buddy Books
An Imprint of Abdo Publishing
abdopublishing.com

abdopublishing.com

Published by Abdo Publishing, a division of ABDO, PO Box 398166, Minneapolis, Minnesota 55439.
Copyright © 2017 by Abdo Consulting Group, Inc. International copyrights reserved in all countries. No part of this book may be reproduced in any form without written permission from the publisher. Big Buddy Books™ is a trademark and logo of Abdo Publishing.

Printed in the United States of America, North Mankato, Minnesota
062016
092016

THIS BOOK CONTAINS
RECYCLED MATERIALS

Design: Sarah DeYoung, Mighty Media, Inc.
Production: Mighty Media, Inc.
Editor: Paige Polinsky
Cover Photograph: Corbis
Interior Photographs: AP Images (pp. 6, 7, 9, 11, 13, 15, 21, 23, 25, 27, 29); Corbis (pp. 6, 19);
    Getty Images (pp. 5, 17)

Cataloging-in-Publication Data

Names: Rumsch, BreAnn., author.
Title: George W. Bush / by BreAnn Rumsch.
Description: Minneapolis, MN : Abdo Publishing, [2017] | Series: United States
    presidents | Includes bibliographical references and index.
Identifiers: LCCN 2015957280 | ISBN 9781680780864 (lib. bdg.) |
    ISBN 9781680775068 (ebook)
Subjects: LCSH: Bush, George, 1946- --Juvenile literature. | Presidents--United
    States--Biography--Juvenile literature. | United States--Politics and
    government--2001-2009--Juvenile literature.
Classification: DDC 973.931/092 [B]--dc23
LC record available at http://lccn.loc.gov/2015957280

Contents

George W. Bush

George W. Bush was the forty-third president of the United States. Before his presidency, Bush served as the governor of Texas.

Bush became president on January 20, 2001. On September 11, the United States faced the worst **terrorist** attacks in its history. Bush took immediate action to protect the country. And in 2003, he led the **Iraq War**.

President Bush was reelected in 2004. Many Americans opposed the war in the Middle East. Yet Bush tried to lead the nation to better times.

Timeline

1946

On July 6, George Walker Bush was born in New Haven, Connecticut.

1994

Bush was elected governor of Texas.

1968

Bush **graduated** from Yale University in New Haven.

2000

Bush was elected the forty-third president of the United States.

2005
Bush began
his second term
as president.
Hurricane
Katrina struck
the Gulf Coast.

2002
Bush passed
the No Child
Left Behind Act.

2003
In March,
the **Iraq War**
began.

2001
On September 11, **terrorists**
attacked the United States.
Bush ordered military
attacks on Afghanistan.

7

Young George

George Walker Bush was born in New Haven, Connecticut, on July 6, 1946. He was the first of Barbara and George H.W. Bush's six children.

In 1948, the Bushes moved to Texas. Sadly, George's sister Robin died in 1953. Her death troubled George for a long time.

George H.W. (*left*) and Barbara (*right*) were pained by Robin's death. George (*center*) tried to cheer them up by telling jokes and playing games.

School Days

In 1959, the Bushes settled in Houston, Texas. Two years later, George's parents sent him to the Phillips **Academy** in Andover, Massachusetts.

At Andover, George missed his family. He also struggled with his lessons. However, he decided to try his best. He studied hard. He also made many new friends.

In 1964, George **graduated** from Phillips Academy. He then entered Yale University in New Haven, Connecticut. There, George studied history.

While in school, George played football, baseball, and basketball. He was also a cheerleader.

Flight School

In 1968, Bush **graduated** from Yale. He then joined the Texas Air National Guard. After two years of flight training, Bush graduated as a **lieutenant**. He continued flying for the Texas Air National Guard.

Meanwhile, Bush had other jobs. He worked on an Alabama **politician**'s campaign for US Senate. He also worked with poor children.

Bush was honorably **discharged** from the Air National Guard in 1973. He then entered Harvard Business School in Boston, Massachusetts.

After basic training, Bush attended flight school at Moody Air Force Base in Valdosta, Georgia.

Oil and Politics

In 1975, Bush **graduated** from Harvard. He returned to Texas. There, Bush worked as a landman in the oil business. Bush asked landowners if oil companies could rent their land to drill for oil.

In 1977, Bush started his own oil company. He called it Arbusto Energy. On November 5, Bush married Laura Welch. Four years later, they welcomed twin girls. They named their daughters Jenna and Barbara.

Jenna (*left*) and Barbara (*right*) helped their father campaign for reelection in 2004.

In 1978, Bush campaigned for a seat in the US House of **Representatives**. But he lost the election. Bush returned to the oil business.

By 1982, oil prices were dropping. Bush's company was losing money. So in 1984, Bush sold the company. Yet he continued to work in the oil business.

Bush returned to **politics** in 1988, when his father ran for president. Bush worked as an adviser and a speechwriter. Bush's father easily won the election.

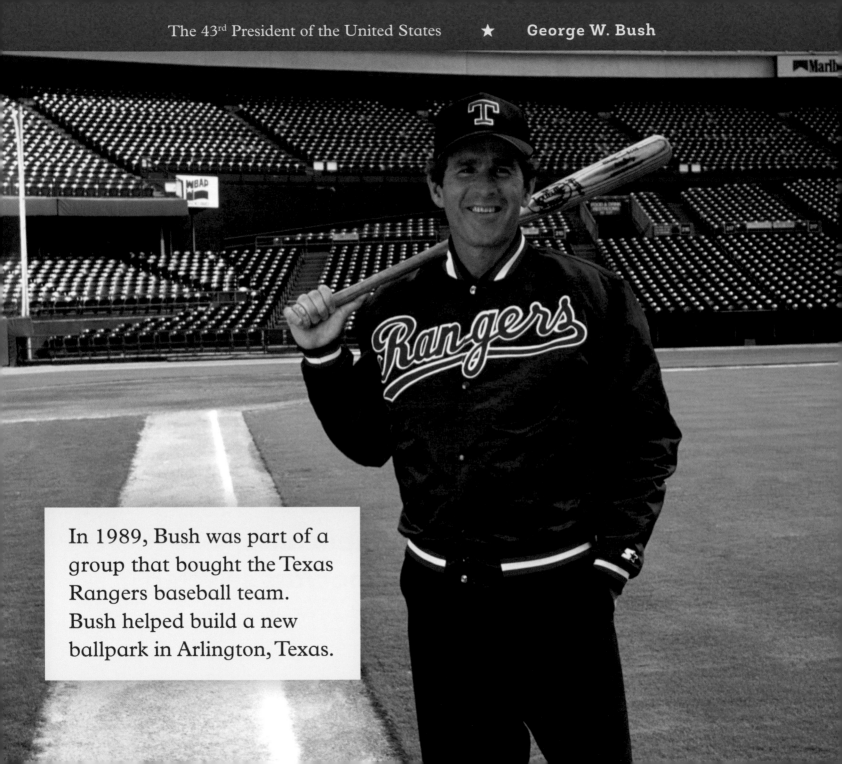

In 1989, Bush was part of a group that bought the Texas Rangers baseball team. Bush helped build a new ballpark in Arlington, Texas.

Governor Bush

In 1994, Bush ran for governor of Texas. He promised to lower crime and increase spending on education. Texans liked Bush's ideas. That year, he won the election.

Governor Bush improved public education. He increased teacher salaries. Bush also cut property taxes. He was reelected in 1998.

In August 2000, the **Republicans** chose Bush to run for president. The **Democrats** selected Vice President Al Gore.

Bush's opposing candidate for governor was Governor Ann Richards. She claimed Bush did not have enough training. But Bush won over Texans.

The 2000 Election

Bush campaigned hard. He promised to improve education. Americans voted on November 7, 2000. But neither Bush nor Gore won enough **electoral votes**.

Whoever won Florida would win the election. Yet, Florida's results were too close to call. The **ballots** were recounted by machine. Bush won.

Gore wanted a recount by hand. But Bush filed several **lawsuits**. On December 12, the **Supreme Court** stopped the recount. The presidency was given to Bush.

Al Gore won more popular votes nationwide. But he still lost the election.

A Bold Leader

On January 20, 2001, Bush entered office. But soon he faced a terrible disaster. On September 11, 2001, **terrorists** attacked the United States. They crashed airplanes in New York City, Washington, DC, and Stonycreek Township, Pennsylvania. About 3,000 people died.

Al-Qaeda was behind the attack. Osama bin Laden led this Afghanistan-based group. Bush asked Afghanistan's government, the Taliban, to give up bin Laden. But the Taliban refused.

Bush toured
the ruins of
the September
11 attacks. He
talked to many
workers who
helped those
suffering.

On October 7, Bush ordered military attacks on Afghanistan. But bin Laden escaped. In November, Bush created the Department of Homeland Security. It was made to guard the United States from **terrorist** attacks.

Meanwhile, Bush worked to improve education. In 2002, he passed the No Child Left Behind Act. It aimed to raise student test scores.

In March 2003, the **Iraq War** began. Bush felt Iraqi president Saddam Hussein was a danger to America. So, the United States **invaded** Iraq.

Iraq's government fell. In May, Bush said that the fighting had ended. However, US troops remained in Iraq. The war was not over.

On October 26, 2001, Bush signed the USA Patriot Act. The law gave government departments more freedom to search for possible terrorists.

Tough Times

In 2004, Bush faced reelection. The war had reduced his popularity. Yet, he beat Massachusetts senator John Kerry.

Bush reentered office in January 2005. That August, **Hurricane** Katrina struck the Gulf Coast. Thousands were killed or left homeless. Bush sent help to the coast. But, many people were upset. They thought the government was too slow to act.

> ★ SUPREME COURT ★
> APPOINTMENTS
>
> **John G. Roberts Jr.:** 2005
>
> **Samuel A. Alito:** 2006

More than 115 million Americans voted in the election between Bush (*left*) and Kerry.

In 2007, Bush tried to send more troops to Iraq. Instead, Congress ordered Bush to remove troops. On May 1, Bush rejected the order.

At this time, the US **economy** was failing. So, in 2008, Bush approved a government plan. It drove Americans to spend more money.

Bush left the White House in January 2009. Meanwhile, his brother Jeb Bush served in **politics**. On June 15, 2015, Jeb entered the presidential race. But he later dropped out.

President George W. Bush faced many difficulties. He fought **terrorism** at home and overseas. Many questioned his choices. But, Bush did his best to serve the nation.

PRESIDENT BUSH'S CABINET

First Term
January 20, 2001–January 20, 2005

- ★ **STATE:** Colin Powell
- ★ **TREASURY:** Paul O'Neill,
  John Snow (from February 3, 2003)
- ★ **ATTORNEY GENERAL:** John Aschcroft
- ★ **INTERIOR:** Gale Norton
- ★ **AGRICULTURE:** Ann M. Veneman
- ★ **COMMERCE:** Don Evans
- ★ **LABOR:** Elaine Chao
- ★ **DEFENSE:** Donald Rumsfeld
- ★ **HEALTH AND HUMAN SERVICES:**
  Tommy Thompson
- ★ **HOUSING AND URBAN DEVELOPMENT:**
  Mel Martinez,
  Alphonso Jackson (from April 1, 2004)
- ★ **TRANSPORTATION:** Norman Mineta
- ★ **ENERGY:** Spencer Abraham
- ★ **EDUCATION:** Rod Paige
- ★ **VETERANS AFFAIRS:** Anthony Principi
- ★ **HOMELAND SECURITY:**
  Tom Ridge (from October 8, 2001)

Second Term
January 20, 2005–January 20, 2009

- ★ **STATE:** Colin Powell,
  Condoleezza Rice (from January 26, 2005)
- ★ **TREASURY:** John Snow,
  Henry M. Paulson Jr. (from July 10, 2006)
- ★ **ATTORNEY GENERAL:** John Ashcroft,
  Alberto Gonzales (from February 3, 2005),
  Michael B. Mukasey (from November 9, 2007)
- ★ **INTERIOR:** Gale Norton,
  Dirk Kempthorne (from May 26, 2006)
- ★ **AGRICULTURE:** Ann M. Veneman,
  Mike Johanns (from January 21, 2005)
- ★ **COMMERCE:** Don Evans,
  Carlos Gutierrez (from February 7, 2005)
- ★ **LABOR:** Elaine Chao
- ★ **DEFENSE:** Donald Rumsfeld,
  Robert Gates (from December 18, 2006)
- ★ **HEALTH AND HUMAN SERVICES:**
  Tommy Thompson,
  Michael O. Leavitt (from January 26, 2005)
- ★ **HOUSING AND URBAN DEVELOPMENT:**
  Alphonso Jackson
- ★ **TRANSPORTATION:** Norman Mineta
- ★ **ENERGY:** Spencer Abraham,
  Samuel W. Bodman (from February 1, 2005)
- ★ **EDUCATION:** Margaret Spellings
- ★ **VETERANS AFFAIRS:** Anthony Principi,
  Jim Nicholson (from February 1, 2005)
- ★ **HOMELAND SECURITY:** Tom Ridge,
  Michael Chertoff (from February 15, 2005)

Office of the President

Branches of Government

The US government has three branches. They are the executive, legislative, and judicial branches. Each branch has some power over the others. This is called a system of checks and balances.

★ Executive Branch

The executive branch enforces laws. It is made up of the president, the vice president, and the president's cabinet. The president represents the United States around the world. He or she also signs bills into law and leads the military.

★ Legislative Branch

The legislative branch makes laws, maintains the military, and regulates trade. It also has the power to declare war. This branch includes the Senate and the House of Representatives. Together, these two houses form Congress.

★ Judicial Branch

The judicial branch interprets laws. It is made up of district courts, courts of appeals, and the Supreme Court. District courts try cases. Sometimes people disagree with a trial's outcome. Then he or she may appeal. If a court of appeals supports the ruling, a person may appeal to the Supreme Court.

Qualifications for Office

To be president, a candidate must be at least 35 years old. The person must be a natural-born US citizen. He or she must also have lived in the United States for at least 14 years.

Electoral College

The US presidential election is an indirect election. Voters from each state choose electors. These electors represent their state in the Electoral College. Each elector has one electoral vote. Electors cast their vote for the candidate with the highest number of votes from people in their state. A candidate must receive the majority of Electoral College votes to win.

Term of Office

Each president may be elected to two four-year terms. The presidential election is held on the Tuesday after the first Monday in November. The president is sworn in on January 20 of the following year. At that time, he or she takes the oath of office.
It states:

I do solemnly swear (or affirm) that I will faithfully execute the office of President of the United States, and will to the best of my ability, preserve, protect and defend the Constitution of the United States.

31

Line of Succession

The Presidential Succession Act of 1947 states who becomes president if the president cannot serve. The vice president is first in the line. Next are the Speaker of the House and the President Pro Tempore of the Senate. It may happen that none of these individuals is able to serve. Then the office falls to the president's cabinet members. They would take office in the order in which each department was created:

Secretary of State

Secretary of the Treasury

Secretary of Defense

Attorney General

Secretary of the Interior

Secretary of Agriculture

Secretary of Commerce

Secretary of Labor

Secretary of Health and Human Services

Secretary of Housing and Urban Development

Secretary of Transportation

Secretary of Energy

Secretary of Education

Secretary of Veterans Affairs

Secretary of Homeland Security

Benefits

★ While in office, the president receives a salary. It is $400,000 per year. He or she lives in the White House. The president also has 24-hour Secret Service protection.

★ The president may travel on a Boeing 747 jet. This special jet is called Air Force One. It can hold 70 passengers. It has kitchens, a dining room, sleeping areas, and more. Air Force One can fly halfway around the world before needing to refuel. It can even refuel in flight!

★ When the president travels by car, he or she uses Cadillac One. It is a Cadillac Deville that has been modified. The car has heavy armor and communications systems. The president may even take Cadillac One along when visiting other countries.

★ The president also travels on a helicopter. It is called Marine One. It may also be taken along when the president visits other countries.

★ Sometimes the president needs to get away with family and friends. Camp David is the official presidential retreat. It is located in Maryland. The US Navy maintains the retreat. The US Marine Corps keeps it secure. The camp offers swimming, tennis, golf, and hiking.

★ When the president leaves office, he or she receives lifetime Secret Service protection. He or she also receives a yearly pension of $203,700. The former president also receives money for office space, supplies, and staff.

PRESIDENTS AND THEIR TERMS

PRESIDENT	PARTY	TOOK OFFICE	LEFT OFFICE	TERMS SERVED	VICE PRESIDENT
George Washington	None	April 30, 1789	March 4, 1797	Two	John Adams
John Adams	Federalist	March 4, 1797	March 4, 1801	One	Thomas Jefferson
Thomas Jefferson	Democratic-Republican	March 4, 1801	March 4, 1809	Two	Aaron Burr, George Clinton
James Madison	Democratic-Republican	March 4, 1809	March 4, 1817	Two	George Clinton, Elbridge Gerry
James Monroe	Democratic-Republican	March 4, 1817	March 4, 1825	Two	Daniel D. Tompkins
John Quincy Adams	Democratic-Republican	March 4, 1825	March 4, 1829	One	John C. Calhoun
Andrew Jackson	Democrat	March 4, 1829	March 4, 1837	Two	John C. Calhoun, Martin Van Buren
Martin Van Buren	Democrat	March 4, 1837	March 4, 1841	One	Richard M. Johnson
William H. Harrison	Whig	March 4, 1841	April 4, 1841	Died During First Term	John Tyler
John Tyler	Whig	April 6, 1841	March 4, 1845	Completed Harrison's Term	Office Vacant
James K. Polk	Democrat	March 4, 1845	March 4, 1849	One	George M. Dallas
Zachary Taylor	Whig	March 5, 1849	July 9, 1850	Died During First Term	Millard Fillmore

PRESIDENT	PARTY	TOOK OFFICE	LEFT OFFICE	TERMS SERVED	VICE PRESIDENT
Millard Fillmore	Whig	July 10, 1850	March 4, 1853	Completed Taylor's Term	Office Vacant
Franklin Pierce	Democrat	March 4, 1853	March 4, 1857	One	William R.D. King
James Buchanan	Democrat	March 4, 1857	March 4, 1861	One	John C. Breckinridge
Abraham Lincoln	Republican	March 4, 1861	April 15, 1865	Served One Term, Died During Second Term	Hannibal Hamlin, Andrew Johnson
Andrew Johnson	Democrat	April 15, 1865	March 4, 1869	Completed Lincoln's Second Term	Office Vacant
Ulysses S. Grant	Republican	March 4, 1869	March 4, 1877	Two	Schuyler Colfax, Henry Wilson
Rutherford B. Hayes	Republican	March 3, 1877	March 4, 1881	One	William A. Wheeler
James A. Garfield	Republican	March 4, 1881	September 19, 1881	Died During First Term	Chester Arthur
Chester Arthur	Republican	September 20, 1881	March 4, 1885	Completed Garfield's Term	Office Vacant
Grover Cleveland	Democrat	March 4, 1885	March 4, 1889	One	Thomas A. Hendricks
Benjamin Harrison	Republican	March 4, 1889	March 4, 1893	One	Levi P. Morton
Grover Cleveland	Democrat	March 4, 1893	March 4, 1897	One	Adlai E. Stevenson
William McKinley	Republican	March 4, 1897	September 14, 1901	Served One Term, Died During Second Term	Garret A. Hobart, Theodore Roosevelt

PRESIDENT	PARTY	TOOK OFFICE	LEFT OFFICE	TERMS SERVED	VICE PRESIDENT
Theodore Roosevelt	Republican	September 14, 1901	March 4, 1909	Completed McKinley's Second Term, Served One Term	Office Vacant, Charles Fairbanks
William Taft	Republican	March 4, 1909	March 4, 1913	One	James S. Sherman
Woodrow Wilson	Democrat	March 4, 1913	March 4, 1921	Two	Thomas R. Marshall
Warren G. Harding	Republican	March 4, 1921	August 2, 1923	Died During First Term	Calvin Coolidge
Calvin Coolidge	Republican	August 3, 1923	March 4, 1929	Completed Harding's Term, Served One Term	Office Vacant, Charles Dawes
Herbert Hoover	Republican	March 4, 1929	March 4, 1933	One	Charles Curtis
Franklin D. Roosevelt	Democrat	March 4, 1933	April 12, 1945	Served Three Terms, Died During Fourth Term	John Nance Garner, Henry A. Wallace, Harry S. Truman
Harry S. Truman	Democrat	April 12, 1945	January 20, 1953	Completed Roosevelt's Fourth Term, Served One Term	Office Vacant, Alben Barkley
Dwight D. Eisenhower	Republican	January 20, 1953	January 20, 1961	Two	Richard Nixon
John F. Kennedy	Democrat	January 20, 1961	November 22, 1963	Died During First Term	Lyndon B. Johnson
Lyndon B. Johnson	Democrat	November 22, 1963	January 20, 1969	Completed Kennedy's Term, Served One Term	Office Vacant, Hubert H. Humphrey
Richard Nixon	Republican	January 20, 1969	August 9, 1974	Completed First Term, Resigned During Second Term	Spiro T. Agnew, Gerald Ford

PRESIDENT	PARTY	TOOK OFFICE	LEFT OFFICE	TERMS SERVED	VICE PRESIDENT
Gerald Ford	Republican	August 9, 1974	January 20, 1977	Completed Nixon's Second Term	Nelson A. Rockefeller
Jimmy Carter	Democrat	January 20, 1977	January 20, 1981	One	Walter Mondale
Ronald Reagan	Republican	January 20, 1981	January 20, 1989	Two	George H.W. Bush
George H.W. Bush	Republican	January 20, 1989	January 20, 1993	One	Dan Quayle
Bill Clinton	Democrat	January 20, 1993	January 20, 2001	Two	Al Gore
George W. Bush	Republican	January 20, 2001	January 20, 2009	Two	Dick Cheney
Barack Obama	Democrat	January 20, 2009	January 20, 2017	Two	Joe Biden

"We seek peace. We strive for peace. And sometimes peace must be defended."

George W. Bush

★ WRITE TO THE PRESIDENT ★

You may write to the president at:
The White House
1600 Pennsylvania Avenue NW
Washington, DC 20500

You may e-mail the president at:
comments@whitehouse.gov

Glossary

academy—a private high school that trains students in a certain field.

al-Qaeda—an Islamic group formed in the 1990s to engage in terrorist activities.

ballot—a piece of paper used to cast a vote.

Democrat—a member of the Democratic political party.

discharged—to be released from military service.

economy—the way that a country produces, sells, and buys goods and services. The study of this is called economics.

electoral vote—a vote cast by a member of the Electoral College for the candidate who received the most popular votes in his or her state.

graduate (GRA-juh-wayt)—to complete a level of schooling.

hurricane—a tropical storm that forms over seawater with strong winds, rain, thunder, and lightning.

invade—to send armed forces into a place, usually to try to take it over.

Iraq War—a conflict begun when the United States and its allies invaded Iraq. After the fall of the Iraqi government, US troops remained in Iraq to help stabilize the new government.

lawsuit—a case held before a court.

lieutenant—an officer of low rank in the armed forces.

politics—the art or science of government. Something referring to politics is political. A person who is active in politics is a politician.

representative—someone chosen in an election to act or speak for the people who voted for him or her.

Republican—a member of the Republican political party.

Supreme Court—the highest, most powerful court of a nation or a state.

terrorist—a person who uses violence to scare or control people or governments.

★ WEBSITES ★

To learn more about the US Presidents, visit **booklinks.abdopublishing.com**. These links are routinely monitored and updated to provide the most current information available.

Index